NEW YEAR'S DAY

Aliki
New Years Day

DATE DUE

JAN 13 '89			

The Library Store   #47-0103

A CROWELL HOLIDAY BOOK

NEW YEAR'S DAY

WRITTEN AND ILLUSTRATED BY
ALIKI

THOMAS Y. CROWELL COMPANY · NEW YORK

L. C. Card AC 67-10069

1   2   3   4   5   6   7   8   9   10

CROWELL HOLIDAY BOOKS

Edited by Susan Bartlett Weber

NEW YEAR'S DAY

LINCOLN'S BIRTHDAY

ST. VALENTINE'S DAY

WASHINGTON'S BIRTHDAY

PURIM

ST. PATRICK'S DAY

PASSOVER

ARBOR DAY

MAY DAY

MOTHER'S DAY

FLAG DAY

THE FOURTH OF JULY

LABOR DAY

THE JEWISH NEW YEAR

COLUMBUS DAY

UNITED NATIONS DAY

HALLOWEEN

ELECTION DAY

THANKSGIVING DAY

HUMAN RIGHTS DAY

HANUKKAH

CHRISTMAS

THE JEWISH SABBATH

SKIP AROUND THE YEAR

There is one night in the year when almost everyone stays up very late. It is December thirty-first, New Year's Eve. This is the night the old year ends and the new year begins.

Even children stay up to welcome the new year. They spend the evening at home with their parents and friends. When midnight finally comes, they make as much noise as they can. They bang on pans and set off alarm clocks. "Happy New Year!" they shout.

Some children go with their families to church. They pray for a happy and peaceful new year.

On December thirty-first many people go to parties to celebrate the arrival
of the new year. There is good food to
eat, music, and dancing. Later in the
evening the guests put on funny paper
hats, and the host gives everyone tin
horns, bells, and noisy rattles.

As midnight draws near, the excitement begins to grow. People look at
their watches. They count off the
minutes.

There are a few last seconds of quiet
waiting. Suddenly the clock strikes
twelve and the new year has come. It is
January first.

Horns blast and noisemakers clang, whir, and ring. Confetti and paper streamers fill the air like a colored snowstorm. People offer toasts to the new year and to each other.

Then someone begins to sing, and all join in. The song they sing is "Auld Lang Syne," an old song about friendship which came to this country from Scotland.

At last, with a final toast, the New Year's Eve party ends. Happy and tired, everyone goes to bed.

Celebration of the new year began thousands of years ago.

At first, the celebrations were held in the spring. The people who lived in those ancient times grew all their own food. The winters were hard, and everyone was filled with joy when the springtime came. Warm sunlight and soft rains brought new crops, which meant new life. It was truly a beginning.

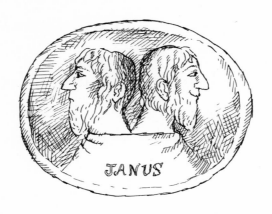

JANUS

Then, in the first century B.C., the Romans made a new calendar. January became the first month of the year, and January first, New Year's Day. Hundreds of years later, most countries in Europe made January first New Year's Day. Americans now celebrate this day, too.

The Romans named January for Janus, the god of all beginnings. Janus had two heads. One looked backward at the old year. The other looked forward to the new year.

The early Roman celebration was wild and joyous. People ate heartily, danced, and gave each other presents.

In the fourth century, the Romans became Christians, and their customs changed. Dancing and parties were thought to be sinful. Instead people fasted and prayed. They asked God to forgive them for their wrongdoings and to help them be good during the new year. New Year's Day became very solemn.

But by the Middle Ages, most people's ideas changed again. They weren't solemn or strict any more. Soon gay celebrations of different kinds began in many countries.

In England, church bells pealed to welcome the new year. When people heard the sound, they opened their doors to let out the spirit of the old year and let in the spirit of the new.

In their homes, English families toasted one another with a spiced drink called wassail. The name came from an ancient toast which meant "to your health."

Poor people roamed the streets carrying empty wassail bowls. They sang New Year's greetings, and were rewarded with food and money to buy their own wassail.

People gave each other gifts again.
During her reign, the queen of England,
Elizabeth I, received so many presents
that the palace cupboards couldn't
hold them all.

Across the Channel from England, the French celebrated New Year's Day with feasting. Dinner guests enjoyed delicious roasts, hams, fresh cheeses, and fruit. They were entertained by masked actors in fancy costumes.

In Holland, the Dutch visited each other on New Year's Day. Much later, when Dutch settlers came to the New World, they brought this friendly custom with them.

As the years passed, each country kept its own special ways of celebrating New Year's Day. Many of the familiar, old customs are still observed today.

In Denmark, boys collect piles of old cups, plates, and jugs. On New Year's Eve they smash them against the doors of friends and neighbors. The more popular a person is, the more dishes and cups are broken at his door.

Children in Belgium make lists of good deeds they will do in the new year. They write the lists on paper decorated with ribbons and flowers, and give them to their parents. The custom of promises for the new year came to America, too. We call them New Year's resolutions.

The Chinese and Japanese get the new year off to a clean start by paying all their bills.

Others believe in different kinds of "clean starts." In Madagascar and Burma, people pour water on their heads to symbolize the washing away of their sins.

In India, Hindus bathe in the Ganges River, or in any nearby river or stream. Their new year still comes in the spring.

In many parts of the world, people clean and paint their houses for the new year.

Some believe the new year holds signs of good or bad luck for them. In Hungary, for good luck, people are supposed to touch a live pig on New Year's Day. In some restaurants, a shoat is let loose at midnight. As it runs squealing around the room, the guests scramble after it.

In Hungary, too, small chimney
sweeps go from house to house. They
sing songs and are rewarded with
money. But while they are busy singing,
everyone tries to steal twigs from their
brooms. The twigs are said to bring
good luck in the new year.

The first person to visit a friend on New Year's Day in Scotland brings good luck, the saying goes. He is called a "first-foot."

In Bulgaria, groups of boys steal through the dark, empty streets, early New Year's Day. Each carries a branch decorated with brightly colored paper flowers.

When the boys come to a house, they knock on the door and sing a song. As soon as the door is opened, they rush in.

Using their branches like magic wands, they tap each member of the family to bring him good luck. Afterward, they are given doughnut-shaped cakes called *kolaches*. With the *kolaches* slipped onto their branches, the boys go merrily on their way.

For the Chinese, the new year is the most important holiday. They have observed it in the same way for centuries.

In the United States today, live many Americans whose parents and grandparents came from China. Some of them still follow the ancient customs of their ancestors.

In China, as well as in Japan, Korea, Burma, and other countries in the Orient, the lunar calendar is used. The twelve months are counted by the moon. When a full moon appears, a new month begins. The Chinese New Year comes on the first day of the first moon. On our calendar, this is in January or February.

Chinese families make sure of good luck in the new year. They seal their doors shut with red good luck papers on New Year's Eve. At midnight, after a quiet greeting, everyone goes to bed. But that quiet greeting is the start of a fifteen-day celebration.

On New Year's Day, the good luck seals are broken. It is another quiet day. And then the fun starts.

The next day everyone puts on the new shoes he has bought and "steps into the new year." Friends visit each other and bring gifts of oranges and candy. They wish one another happiness and a long life.

Children and grown-ups fill the streets on the days that follow. Musicians sing and play their instruments. Actors give a pageant called the Dragon Play.

On the fifteenth day is the colorful Feast of Lanterns. Streets and houses are decorated with paper lanterns of all sizes and shapes. Children and their parents parade through the darkness with still more lanterns, each with a lighted candle inside.

Then the most exciting part of the parade appears. It is a huge dragon made of bamboo, silk, and paper. The dragon is a symbol of strength and goodness. Sometimes it is so long a hundred boys are needed to carry it.

As the dragon passes, the watching crowd sets off loud bursts of fire-crackers. With that, the celebration of the new year comes to an end.

The many different ways of celebrating the new year have been passed from people to people, from country to country, over thousands of years. But whatever the country, whatever the custom, certain things seem to be the same. We all like to celebrate a new beginning. We like to have a good time and to remember our friends with greetings and with gifts. We like to make a fresh start and resolve to do better in the year to come.

Then when the excitement of the holiday is over, we pause for a quiet moment to wonder what the new year will bring.

ABOUT THE AUTHOR-ILLUSTRATOR

Versatility is the key to Aliki's career as a commercial artist and a children's book author and illustrator. Besides her art work, she loves music, books, and making dolls.

Mrs. Franz Brandenberg in private life, Aliki grew up in Philadelphia and attended the Museum College of Art in that city. An avid traveler, she has visited much of the United States and Europe.

Aliki, her husband, and their two children live in New York City.